YOUNG LIONS OF JUDAH

YOUNG LIONS OF JUDAH

Mike Evans with Bob Summers

LOGOS INTERNATIONAL
Plainfield, New Jersey

YOUNG LIONS OF JUDAH

Copyright © 1974 by Logos International
185 North Avenue, Plainfield, N.J. 07060
All Rights Reserved
Printed in the United States of America
Library of Congress Catalog Card Number: 73-84781
ISBN: 0-88270-059-6 (paper)

CONTENTS

Introduction: A New Genesis	vii
In the Beginning	1
And the Earth Was without Form *Arthur Katz*	7
God Painted Me into a Corner *Sid Roth*	13
Let There Be Light *Hal Sacks*	31
Jesus Made Me Jewish *Mike Evans*	37
The God Who Led Abraham *Sarah Schneider [pseudonym]*	43
There Was This Girl *Jeffrey H. Allen*	53

My Kinsman According to the Flesh *Menaham Ben-Hayim*	69
I was "Gay," But Now I'm Happy *Alan Greenberg*	81
The Lost Sheep of the House of Israel *Abraham Eilezer*	87
And God Saw That It Was Good *Anne Goldman* [*pseudonym*]	93
The Movement Spreads	97
An Afterword: Jewish Culture and Identity *Joseph Finkelstein*	105

INTRODUCTION
A NEW GENESIS

OUT of the contemporary malaise of apathy, existentialism, civil disobedience, and the drug scene, a strange specter has emerged. Thousands of young Jews are meeting around the country in groups to sing and pray in the name of "Yeshua" (Jesus). Nor are these groups insular and self-contained. Observers of the more familiar "Jesus movement" are beginning to note a steadily increasing number of Jewish believers in both the rank and file and the leadership.

On the West Coast, rabbis have decried the defection of numerous Jewish college students to Jesus, while a former rabbi named Esses is now lecturing to a large congregation of Christians near Disneyland. Not far away, at Costa Mesa's Calvary Chapel, the most popular Jesus songs of the youthful, one-thousand-member congregation are written and sung by a Jewish girl. The Hidden Manna, a coffeehouse that is one of the centers for Chicago's Jesus People, is operated by Jews who acclaim the Nazarene as Israel's Messiah.

Florida boasts a full-fledged Messianic synagogue where the once hated Name is exalted as the fulfillment of God's promises to Abraham and his descendants. A similar congregation of Jews, organized along less traditional lines, meets in Philadelphia. One of the most ardent spokesmen for the movement, a former Marxist from Brooklyn, has established the headquarters of his center for Messianic Judaism within a half hour of New York City.

These phenomena seem to have arisen independently, but a constant refrain is heard from their spokesmen in every part of the country: these Jews have not ceased to be Jews. Their allegiance to Jesus does not, they claim, constitute a defection from Judaism; on the contrary, it is the fulfillment of all that their ancient heritage promised. Their radical commitment to the Galilean rabbi has made them, they proclaim, *Messianic Jews*.

In the face of these claims, the reaction of

the Jewish establishment has been hostile. To them, this "new Judaism" is but the old Christianity, and they are not impressed.

The establishment and incredible maintenance of a Jewish political state at the eastern end of the Mediterranean had infused new energy into an exhausted and decimated Judaism through the fifties and sixties, and had seemed the final culmination of the Jewish destiny. But now this. What could it mean? Just as the remnant of this ancient race was gaining new stature and confidence in the integrity of its religious heritage, how could something like *this* happen?

Chagrined but undissuaded, these remarkably zealous Messianic Jews assert their claims and reinforce them from the Old Testament. In the books of Isaiah, Ezekiel, and Daniel, and on through the minor prophets, they find Scripture to support their cause. Jeremiah, they are quick to note, spoke clearly of a new covenant that God would establish with His people (31:31-34). The Jewish Jesus children identify the fulfillment of Jeremiah's prophecy with the covenant of which Jesus spoke during the Seder He shared with His close disciples on the eve of His execution (Mark 14:12-25).

All this has had an unnerving effect on Jewish leaders. They have attacked the Jesus Jews as traitors whose proposals would lead to the absorption of the American Jewish community by the Gentile milieu. Militant Jewish Defense League leaders have viewed them as pernicious, albeit unwitting, allies of anti-Semites, playing into the hands of Soviet policies. So far, the hostility has been largely verbal, but a mood of physical violence hangs heavy in the air as neither side relents and nerves grow taut.

The Messianic Jews protest that theirs is not a work of proselytizing but of evangelizing. To proselytize is to persuade a person to leave one belief and enter another, but to evangelize is to announce the good news that the old promises have been kept and made good to a waiting people. "In other words," declares a young Jew in Dallas, "we are not trying to convert a Jew out of Judaism into Christianity. We are not converting him at all. He is a Jew and always will be. We are merely showing him how he might fulfill his Judaism in Yeshua as Messiah, to be a spiritual Jew."

The conflict has yet to be fully joined; what has happened so far amounts to nothing more than a preliminary skirmish. The future promises to be increasingly hazardous for those Messianic Jews who are committed to a stance of militant non-violence. While strongly asserting their authentic Jewishness, they are among the most uncompromising of the Jesus People. They regard their real battle as being drawn along spiritual and not physical lines. This means that the resources on their side of the struggle will be prayer, fasting, a pure heart, a clear conscience, and a genuine faith (I Tim. 1:5).

Just prior to Passover, 1973, the first Messianic Discipleship Conference was held in Plainfield, New Jersey. Young Jewish disciples of Christ gathered from various parts of the Northeast, the upper Midwest, and even from Israel. The traditional Jesus People trappings of beards, blue jeans, and smiling faces were much in evidence, along with Star of David medallions. Besides the familiar hymns and choruses, the conferees sang a song with a lilting Hebraic melody called "Baruch ha Shem ha' Mashiach Yeshua" ("Bless the Name of the Messiah Jesus").

Speakers at the conference tended to minimize the harshness of their conflict with the Jewish establishment, and spoke frequently and fondly of "our people." The emphasis was on the disciple's responsibility to permit God to make radical changes in his life, changes that would rid him of self-righteousness, arrogance, and the like, in order to let him be more thoroughly conformed to the image of Christ (Rom. 8:29). Nearly a dozen men and women were baptized in water during the three-day weekend meeting, and the conference concluded with a full-fledged Seder on the afternoon of Passover eve. Many of the conferees then left to participate in family Seders in their own homes.

The object of this book is to permit the reader a behind-the-scenes look at the personalities and events of the Messianic Jewish movement that has generated so much controversy across our land, to show who they are who have been dubbed *Young Lions of Judah.*

IN THE BEGINNING

IN THE early 1960s, a tremendous new surge of the Holy Spirit swept over the world. Denominational walls, which had for a long time divided Christians from one another, began to tumble. People of diverse persuasions were suddenly fellowshiping and praying together. This many-faceted movement bore various names, but one name—a Jewish one—stuck: Pentecostal.

Every area of Christendom seemed astir. This was the period of Pope John XXIII and the Vatican Council on Ecumenism. Both the Pope and his Council were forerunners of a refreshing new movement within world Catholicism: the Catholic Pentecostals.

While on his way to attend the Vatican Council, David du Plessis a Pentecostal clergyman, stopped by to visit the distinguished Swiss theologian, Karl Barth. Even the aging Barth was excited. He was moved to prophesy of the vast new outpouring of the Holy Spirit upon *all* flesh: "God is not going to isolate or separate any. He is going to let His Spirit reach everybody."

At this time, John Osteen, a Southern Baptist pastor, was experiencing a tremendous personal visitation of the Holy Spirit. At a large Full Gospel Businessmen's Fellowship convention in Denver, Colorado, he prophesied that the next great visitation of God's Spirit *would be among the Jews!* Everywhere, similar utterances were being heard.

All the facts, however, seemed to belie these prophecies. Since the end of the first century, the number of Jews who called Jesus their Messiah had been few and easily numbered. And this in spite of the fact that the first Jesus movement began among the Jews. Everything about it was Jewish—its worship was directly modeled on the form of worship found in the synagogue, and its adherents were virtually indistinguishable from members of the Jewish community. In fact, early Christianity was regarded by the Roman authorities as a Jewish sect.

But this changed with the passage of time. Orthodox Judaism displayed implacable hostility toward the followers of Jesus, thus making it impossible for these early Christians to exist in a strictly Jewish milieu. And as the movement spread throughout the Mediterranean world, it gradually took an entirely new form. The New Testament was written neither in Hebrew nor Aramaic, but in Koine, a Greek vernacular dialect that was the *lingua franca* of the ancient world. Inevitably, the Jewish origins of Christianity were blurred.

An instance of this is found in the very name "Christ." In Hebrew, the name of the founder of Christianity would be *Yeshua ha' Mashiach*, "Jesus the Anointed One." The equivalent term in Greek for "Anointed One" is *Christos*. And since the Good News was spread in Greek, it followed that Jesus' Jewish identity was submerged.

This, for better or worse, was the direction that early Christianity took. Though the source of both its form and substance was Jewish, official Jewish hostility to Christianity served virtually to expunge all traces of its Jewish origin. So foreign did Christianity become that no Jew would have anything to do with it.

It did not have to be this way. Anyone who

has ever read the letters of Paul cannot help but weep for the past nineteen hundred years of the almost complete absence of Jews and their heritage from the Church. The message of salvation, Paul stressed, was "to the Jew first."

> For I am not ashamed of the gospel of Christ: for it is the power of God unto salvation to every one that believeth; to the Jew first, and also to the Greek. (Rom. 1:16)

The Jewish rejection of the Gospel weighed heavily upon Paul's soul. His writings speak of that agony:

> I say the truth in Christ, I lie not, my conscience also bearing me witness in the Holy Ghost, That I have great heaviness and continual sorrow in my heart. For I could wish that myself were accursed from Christ for my brethren, my kinsmen according to the flesh: Who are Israelites; to whom pertaineth the adoption, and the glory, and the covenants, and the giving of the law, and the service of God, and the promises. (Rom. 9:1-4)

Yet it was none other than Paul himself who spoke of the hardening Jewish opposition to Jesus:

> (According as it is written, God hath given them the spirit of slumber, eyes that they should not

see, and ears that they should not hear;) unto this day. (Rom. 11:8)

Paul believed that through the Jews' fall, "salvation is come unto the Gentiles, for to provoke them to jealousy" (Rom. 11:11). But he quickly adds that he is not satisfied with the situation:

> Now if the fall of them be the riches of the world, and the diminishing of them the riches of the Gentiles; how much more their fulness? (Rom. 11:12)

Jesus had earlier prefaced His plea for acceptance with this warning to the Jews: "Ye shall seek me, and shall not find me" (John 7:34).

John, a leading spokesman of the first-century Jews for Jesus, wearied at being persecuted by other Jews. He flatly stated that his Jewish detractors were not worthy of the title of *Jew*. In the Revelation, he quoted the Lord as saying,

> Behold, I will make them of the synagogue of Satan,* which say they are Jews, and are not,

---

* This is a harsh play on words, for the official title over the door of the Jewish synagogue read "Synagogue of the Lord."

but do lie; behold, I will make them to come and worship before thy feet, and to know that I have loved thee. (Rev. 3:9)

For centuries, therefore, the Jew was a rare sight at Christian gatherings. Indeed, the very name of Christ became repulsive to the Jew. To him, Christ was the originator of Christianity—and Christianity came quickly to be associated with anti-Semitism and persecution. The Jew saw himself as being a Jew *by birth*: thus all other western men were born *Christian*.

A change in attitude was bound to come, however. Spokesmen among the Pentecostals, charismatics, and Jesus People have been boisterously vocal in repudiating the link between Christianity and western materialism. It is in this that one area of their strength lies. They are aware of the transience of civilization and its security; their priorities do not take such things as privilege, convenience, or security into consideration. Thus they are estranged from the world in which they live.

With this estrangement, the Jew can easily identify. He is quite used to being on the outside, looking in.

Arthur Katz was one such Jew.

AND THE EARTH WAS WITHOUT FORM

Arthur Katz

ARTHUR KATZ came up the hard way. If it were not for the big smile across his rugged face, this man's gaze might betray the scars of dirty Brooklyn streets, Jewish ghettos, and cold, lonely nights.

Life for Art, as his friends know him, was no more than a circus of absurdities. He *hated*. This lonely Jew hated everything except his Jewishness. But, paradoxically, Art was not a religious man. His Jewishness was to him a source of historical pride. He despised rabbis and ministers. To him religion was a rubber crutch for a crippled man. It was absurd— man's futile attempt to fill his existential void.

At the University of California's Berkeley campus, Art found at least some sense of meaning. He carried the banner, in his own words, "for all the appropriate student causes." Determined to champion the underdog, Art became a spokesman for Marxism. His goal was to build a better world through universal education. But his idealism soon collapsed in the face of reality. When he became a teacher in a public school, he found that his students were not in the least interested in the lofty philosophical ideologies that were so dear to him. They were much more concerned with acne, hot rods, and tight sweaters. A couple of years with teenage students of history was all Art could take.

He resigned his teaching post to set out on a search for life. He didn't know where he was going. He only knew he had to go. In his wandering quest, Art took passage on a ship for Europe. There he took to the land, wanting to visit the cultural centers he had held so dear. His wrinkled old knapsack across his back, his face often unshaven, Art must have looked more like a desperado than a serious intellectual seeking a meaning for his existence.

While in Europe, Katz developed an interest in the works of Carl Jung. Jung's psychiatry and Christian apologetics not only fascinated him but pricked his conscience.

Something else happened in Europe. He met two genuinely loving and humble Christians. Art could not explain away their love and joy. Nor could he argue with it.

While a deckside passenger bound from Italy to Greece, Art borrowed a New Testament and began to read it in earnest. On deck it was misty, cold and dark, so Art had to sit by a porthole and read by the light that came from the ship's first-class cabins. From these cabins also came the sounds of music and laughter. The smell of fine foods filled the air. Unaware of Art's quest, and frivolously unconcerned with the deckside passengers outside, the beautiful people dined and partied in first-class elegance.

"We lost souls outside—" Art later told me, "imagine our vanity: we were seeking the answers to life. But we were on the outside looking in. The people inside—they could have cared less about life."

It was in those lonely moments that the New Testament began to come to life for Art. He began to find in the New Testament Jesus, his kind of hero. Could He be the Messiah? At least, thought Art, this Jesus would have had time for the world's rejects and misfits.

But when Art finally reached Jerusalem, the goal of his travels, he found no encouragement. There he encountered people of all educational levels—even Martin Buber the famous Jewish philosopher. Most of these people, with the best of intentions, steered the young seeker's thoughts away from the Gospels. But one final day, while he was on his way to visit a Hasidic community, Art got on the wrong bus. When he realized his mistake, he got off at the next stop. Since he was not familiar with the section of Jerusalem in which he found himself, he stepped inside a bookstore to ask directions. A kindly lady answered his questions. Then, as Art was leaving, he noticed a book by Carl Jung. Suddenly he realized that all the books that were displayed throughout the little shop concerned Jesus and Christian themes.

"What is this place?" Art quickly demanded.

"This is a Messianic Assembly," the lady replied with a glowing smile. "We are all Jews who have accepted Jesus as our Messiah. We have a small chapel in the back for prayer and study."

Describing his reaction, Art said, "Something strangely broke in my heart. In the same moment an inward voice calling me by name commanded me to remain: 'Art, you are not to leave.' I had never before heard or believed the possibility of hearing such a still, small voice, and would have been suspicious of any who claimed such an experience. Instead, in that moment, I intuitively recognized the voice of Him who called to Abraham and invited fellow Jews centuries later to leave their boats and nets to follow Him. It was the voice of Him above who had the right to command my Jewish loyalties and life."

Art asked to stay. And permission was gladly granted. For several days he remained in that little meeting room, poring through book after book. He had long discussions about Jesus with the other Jews of the Assembly. They prayed with him and for him. Art's reaction?

"At the conclusion of my stay, I was utterly bewildered. I had received an intensive, enormous overview of the Bible. For four days, prophetic Scriptures had been opened to me, but I just could not seem to put it together in my mind. I was so proud of my intelligence—but it was incapable of saving me. In that last night, through a troubled sleep, the Lord began to put the pieces into place, and I awoke the next morning in a state of complete peace and calm. My years of vexation and striving were at an end. 'Rena,' I said to the lady I'd first met there, 'I believe I understand.' And the lady fell to her knees and worshiped God."

In the years since that moment, Arthur Katz has become a well-known spokesman for Messianic Judaism. He is a familiar visitor to college campuses and youth gatherings. His book, *Ben Israel*, is a best seller. Many Christian publications have carried his editorials.

"In the younger Jews of my generation," Art told me, "there has developed a longing for the supernatural and personal God of Abraham. That we might find Him is the promise of Jeremiah's prophecy:

> And ye shall seek me, and find me, when ye shall search for me with all your heart. And I will be found of you, saith the Lord. (Jer. 29:13-14)

GOD PAINTED ME INTO A CORNER

Sid Roth

MY parents gave me love—maybe too much. They loved God in their way. In fact, God was my father's whole life. He made sure I went to Hebrew School, observed all the holidays, and at thirteen was a bar mitzvah.° But I saw in him what Isaiah meant when he prophesied from God, "This people draw near with their words And honor Me with their lipservice, But they remove their hearts far from Me, And their reverence for Me consists of tradition learned by rote" (Isa. 29:13 NASB).

I'm not saying I was an atheist, but I never

° This Hebrew term means "son of righteousness" and refers to the rite of initiation of adolescents into the adult religious community.

saw or heard or thought about the God that my father loved. Judaism looked so hypocritical to me. It was a culture based on tradition and heritage and pride—centered on what we could see or touch or feel rather than what we could not see. Most of my Jewish friends went to the synagogue out of respect for their parents or to set an example for their children, but their hearts were far from God. I remember being forced to sit in the synagogue all day hearing words in Hebrew that I didn't understand. What torture! But I did my duty, as perhaps my father did and his father before him.

A real crisis occurred when I fell in love with a girl who was not Jewish. I never once considered that I should become a Christian; this was beyond my comprehension. There is something ingrained in the Jew that makes the name Jesus repulsive. Even when Joy said she would convert to Judaism, my parents still tried to change my mind. My father was shattered over the marriage, but time is a great healer of wounds, and after a while Joy was accepted into the family.

Joy and I were in our early twenties when we were married. Even though we loved each other, both of us were selfish, conceited, and frustrated. We were headed toward divorce from the first day. Seven years and one child later, we separated.

I was hurt inside about the separation, but another part of me was happy. After all, I had really never had a chance to know many women and have fun. What else was there in life?

I moved into an apartment with a bachelor—a real swinger. Before he asked me to live with him, he interviewed me. His first question was, "Do you mind if my girl friend stays with me?" My answer was, "Yes, because she isn't staying with me." We laughed, and I passed the test.

That year, I can never forget.

I had always been interested in the occult realm—astrology, fortune-telling, handwriting analysis, hypnosis, reincarnation, communicating with the dead, magic, Ouija boards, and psychic powers. The occult held a fascination that was beyond a mere hobby or interest. A real force drew me toward these areas. I couldn't go by a fortune-teller's studio without stopping for a reading. When I found one who could really predict the future, I consulted him about every major decision.

For eight years, I had been in the investment

business, and although I was successful by worldly standards, I had been with eight different firms over that period. At the time, I thought I kept switching jobs in order to make more money. Now I know I switched because I was unhappy and didn't know what I was searching for.

One day, Jim, a man who worked for me, told me, "My friend in New Jersey just took a course that allows him to know things that he has no natural means of knowing. I'll give you an example: you can tell him the name of someone he doesn't know, and he will tell you what's wrong with that person physically, and many other things about that person. The course takes only one week, and I can assure you he never had this ability before. By the way, if you can't do at least what he can, the course is free!"

I was so interested that the next day I drove to New Jersey to talk to Jim's friend. I gave him what I considered an acid test. I told him the name of a man who had recently shot himself in the head and had survived. He had no way of knowing this person, and what he said both shocked and excited me:

"I see a light going toward this man's head—

it's entering into his head—it seems to be shattering. Could this be a bullet?" My one driving thought was how soon could I take the course.

During the first two days of class, we learned how to relax. We were told that we had to lower the speed of our brain waves to the frequency that occurs while we sleep. After achieving this, we were told to imagine that we had a counselor in our head. This counselor would answer any question we asked and perform any test we desired.

By the end of the week, as the class drew to a close, we were all excited, eager to see if mind control would work for us. We divided into groups of four, and I was given the name of someone I didn't know. A vision formed in my head of a woman with something wrong with one breast. I blurted it out: "Could she have cancer of the breast?"

"That's right! Bravo! You can do it, Sid!"

The next day at work, my boss came in to see me. Before he could say anything, I ushered him into my office and told him to sit down. Then I asked him to give me the name of someone I didn't know who was sick. He looked at me as if he thought *I* was sick, but decided to humor me and mentioned his father's name. I closed my eyes. They began to flicker as I lowered the speed of my brain waves. Then both of my arms started to shake. While I was trying to figure out what was happening, my boss said, "That's exactly what my father does!"

I asked, "Could he have Parkinson's disease?" I didn't know what the disease was, but the name just came to me.

"Yes, that's it!" said my boss, excitedly. Then I told him that I didn't have to shake my arms anymore. At that, he volunteered that yesterday his father started taking L-Dopa, which had successfully controlled his shaking.

Wow! Was I excited! Here was real power!

The more I experimented, the more uses I found for my new ability. One day when I was lost in the park, I merely said, "Counselor, direct me home." I was directed to make turns on unfamiliar streets and found myself at home in record time. If I needed a parking space, even in the most difficult circumstances, all that was necessary was for me to ask that a space be available. It didn't matter how impossible the situation. Once we went to a stage show at the National Theater in Washington, D.C., and I got a parking space right in front of the theater just five minutes before curtain!

God Painted Me into a Corner 19

How about people? Could I make people do things as easily as I created parking spaces and perceived information at a distance? Yes, yes, yes. Almost as quickly as I thought of something I wanted, people began doing my will. If I wanted money, women, or increased sales, all I had to do was ask.

About this time, I began thinking about starting my own business. Shortly thereafter, an attorney whom I knew only casually came into my office and offered me a free office, phone, and secretary! His motivation was that he had extra space anyway, and I might be able to sell stock in his company for him. He also told me that a friend of his whom I didn't know had told him I would soon come into the Kingdom of Heaven. I smiled, thinking about the generous offer generated by my ability—and only half-thinking about God.

The next week at a meeting of graduates of the mind course, a lady walked up to me with a sealed envelope. She said, "Sid, if you promise not to open this envelope for one year, you can have it. It's a prophecy about your life."

I countered quickly, "Will you let me open it if I tell you the prophecy?" After her yes, I told her that it probably said I'd do something on the order of Billy Graham. She got so excited that everyone in the room looked up.

"Open the prophecy," she said. The message was basically that organized churches were going against God's will and that I would destroy many of them. What a wild idea for a nice Jewish boy! Visions of Elmer Gantry danced in my head.

About this time, I was getting a great deal of unsolicited advice about my broken marriage. My psychic friends were against my returning to my wife, but a still, still feeling inside me said, "Go back to her." Joy had decided she definitely wanted to try again. But because of my friends and new business activities, I put off making a decision.

I resigned from my job and set up shop in my friend's free office space. Then God started painting me into a corner.

I didn't know it at the time, but Jim Fisk, the president of the computer company that gave me office space, was one of those Jesus fanatics. You know the type—the ones who raise their hands over their heads and get real loud praising God.

Jim had all the Jesus People in town trooping through his offices, and they had prayer meetings morning, noon, and night. And guess who they were praying and fasting for—me!

In spite of all the confusion that I caused in those meetings, they still kept inviting me back for more. They were good, honest people, and although I thought they were kooks, I still liked them. For example, I had lunch one day with Bruce Jackson, and he said, "Let's not talk business. Let's just get acquainted. I'm interested in you as a person. I'd like to share Jesus with you." This type of love of God I had never seen before. It got to me.

Then he said something that caused me to resent him just a little. He said that God frowned on my involvement with mind control, and he asked me to read what God says in Deuteronomy 18:10-12.

There I read that it was an abomination before God to fool around with fortune-telling, witchcraft, psychic phenomena, dead spirits, ESP and the like.

In spite of my skepticism, I was bothered enough to go to the top mind control instructor in the area and ask the question, "Where does my power come from?" Though the Bible said it was evil, I didn't believe it, and I did want to get those religious fanatics off my back. But I hit a dead end. The instructor didn't know where the power came from. This bothered me more than what the Bible said. He suggested I ask his boss the same question.

So the next week I drove to Pennsylvania to question one of the top mind control people in the country. I asked Gene Griffin, a Bible teacher, to go with me on this trip. I figured that I'd just sit back and let the two of them argue it out. But Gene prayed to God and refused to come along. This annoyed me. If he was so all-fired interested in my relation to God, why couldn't he accompany me on this trip? The whole way up, I kept telling myself that I hoped the Bible and my so-called friends were wrong. I enjoyed using the power I had, and I didn't want to give it up. By the time I arrived at my destination, I had convinced myself that what I wanted to believe was true.

My first question to the instructor was, "What do you think of the Bible?"

He said, "It's a good book, but there are many good books."

My second question was, "Do you believe in evil?"

He said, "There is no such thing as evil. Evil is only in man's mind. If you don't think about evil, there is none." Then he said, "Sid, if you ever have a problem, just think of me, and I'll know your problem and answer you by my thoughts."

I was convinced. This power was good. In fact, as I was driving home, I thought about going into mind control full time—teaching the subject.

Several days later, I went to a mind control meeting and asked one of the most experienced students to ask his counselor what I would be doing one year from that day. He closed his eyes and asked his counselor the question. His counselor not only refused to answer, but started to curse him. Stupefied, he said, "This is the first time he's ever been anything but a perfect gentleman with me."

I couldn't understand why my friend's counselor wouldn't answer him. Did he see my death or something so awful that he couldn't answer? I began to be afraid.

About this time, I found that whenever I had a question, all I had to do was open a dictionary at random and the word to which I pointed would be the exact answer to my question. For instance, I experimented by asking, "What color is the sky?" The word I pointed to was "blue."

Then I felt like going to the dictionary when

I didn't have a question! The first word I pointed to was "refrain." I wrote it down, and I also wrote the words that followed on a pad of paper. Finally I read the completed message: "Refrain from this sinful dictionary."

I crumpled up the piece of paper, and threw it in the trash can. Later, I told Gene Griffin about the incident. Before I could finish, he started to praise God. I left the office shaken, trying to figure out what was going on. Was God mad at me for using other sources of power than His?

Several days later, after I had talked myself out of this latest encounter with God, I went to a mind control meeting and all of us went into meditation. This time, something new happened. I saw myself come out of myself. I asked the woman next to me what that meant, and she was excited.

"You've just found your astral soul," she said. "Now you can have anything you want. You now have greater power than you ever dreamed possible." My excitement cooled rapidly at her next statement: "But, Sid, let me warn you— Never go too far with your astral soul. Because sometimes you can't find your way back to your body."

God Painted Me into a Corner 25

Sudden fear gripped me, but it faded when I resolved on a simple precaution. I would never go more than a few feet from my body. That way, I *couldn't* get lost.

The following week, I went to another occult meeting, the Inner Peace movement. The lecturer spoke on the subject of astral projection. Among other things, he said that every time we sleep, our astral soul goes for a walk. Real fear clutched at me again. When I was conscious, I had complete control over where my soul wandered, but while I was asleep, I had no control. I had the most gruesome thoughts you can imagine. But I was still unrepentant, and God continued to paint me deeper into that corner.

The next day, when I went to my office, Jim Fisk looked at me and said, "Sid, you look like you have a case of spiritual neurosis." I was certainly not interested in discussing anything like that. I left early and went to a bookstore to get something to read. A book caught my eye. It was called *The Bible, the Supernatural, and the Jews*, and it was written by McCandlish Phillips. I started reading the book, and I just couldn't put it down. It said it was an abomination for anyone to fool with the occult, but it was worse for a Jew, because the Jews are

God's Chosen People. And when a Jew sins, God judges him more strictly than He would judge a Gentile. The book went on to name prominent Jews who had lost their lives by doing exactly what I was doing!

At this point, I was afraid to go to sleep for fear that my soul would leave and not be able to find its way back to my body. What could I do? To whom could I go? The mind control instructor? He didn't even know where the power was coming from. My wife? My rabbi? My parents? A psychiatrist? They wouldn't even understand what I was talking about.

Was it too late to turn to Jesus? I didn't know.

I ran to a jewelry store and bought a mezuzah to put around my neck. I asked my wife to pray to Jesus for me. Though she considered herself an agnostic at the time, she had been raised a Baptist, so at least she knew this Jesus. When I asked her to pray for me to Jesus, that was all the opening He needed. I had finally approached Him as honestly as I could. That's all He requires.

That night I put my Bible under my pillow and asked Jesus to get me out of the mess I had got myself into, because no one else could.

When my head hit the pillow, I didn't know whether I would live through the night.

The next morning, I died and was reborn—I died to sin and was made alive to God. As Paul says in Galatians 2:20, "I have been crucified with Christ; it is no longer I who live, but Christ who lives in me; and the life I now live in the flesh, I live by faith in the Son of God, who loved me, and gave himself for me" (RSV).

What peace and love and happiness I experienced that morning! It was great to be alive, really alive as you can be only when you personally know Jesus. I went to my office and called Don Tobias. Don was president of a computer company. I had read about his healing ministry in the newspaper.

Instead of talking to Don about the Lord, I tried to interest him in a business deal. He said that he would stop by my office the next day. When he came in, before I could talk business, he was praying for my short leg to grow out. There was a quarter of an inch difference between them, and I watched my leg grow until both were exactly the same length. Then I said, "Don, I'd like to accept Jesus."

His face beamed, and he led me in a simple

prayer of salvation. Although I had had the experience of being born again the day before, I felt it was necessary for me to formally accept Jesus in front of a witness. I was *proud* to be a child of God.

From that day, God began to pour out blessings upon me. My marriage was made whole! Before I accepted Jesus, there was no way I could have returned to my wife, and if I had, there was no way the marriage could possibly have worked.

Almost simultaneously, God had a company offer me a job at twice the amount of money they would normally offer.

Don't get the wrong idea. I'm not saying that just because you turn to Jesus you'll be rich and be free of problems. But the greatest wealth in all the world is the peace of knowing and serving God. Problems are easy to bear when we know that God is in control.

Some time after my turning to Jesus, I received a phone call. "Hi, Sid, this is Bruce," said the voice on the other end of the line. "We need your help with a newspaper article." A reporter from the Washington *Daily News* wanted to do a feature article on white-collar Jesus freaks. I told Bruce that the reporter could call me, but I was hesitant about publicity for myself. My father didn't know of my commitment to Jesus. He came from the old-country Orthodox Judaism, and "Christian" was a dirty word to him. Still, I felt the article was of God, and when the reporter came to my office, I gave him the interview. When I found out he was a Jew, I was less interested in answering his questions than in telling him about Jesus.

Several times he gave me a funny look and said, "Just answer my questions. I'm conducting the interview."

When he asked me about my parents, I agreed to tell him about them for his benefit, but got him to promise that he wouldn't put the information in the paper.

"I promise," he said.

But when the interview appeared in the paper, my words about my parents were on the front page. I felt sick.

I called my mother to apologize, and she said, "How could you have done this to your father?" She was heartbroken, and so was I.

After I hung up, I prayed to my perfect Father to be gentle with my earthly father. God heard my prayer—and performed a miracle.

My father never saw that article, in spite of the fact that it appeared on the front page of a major local newspaper. Praise God. Today, my father knows I believe in Jesus.

You know, if a Jew is an atheist, he is still considered a Jew. But if a Jew believes in Jesus, he is not considered a Jew. Ironic, isn't it? Today I feel more Jewish than ever before, because in addition to a rich heritage and culture, I've found God. How could it be otherwise?

Jesus was born of Jewish parents and preached only to Jews. His first disciples were all Jews, and when He died on the cross, the inscription read, "King of the Jews." If Jesus was the Jewish Messiah, then why am I not a Jew if I believe in Him? The only reason I didn't believe in Him for the first thirty years of my life was because some ancestor whose name I don't know decided Jesus wasn't the Messiah. Suppose this same ancestor had believed that Jesus was the Messiah? It would be silly for me to accept or reject Jesus based on his decision. Every Jew and Gentile must decide for himself.

LET THERE BE LIGHT

Hal Sacks

HAL SACKS, a ruddy-faced young Jew with a debonair West Coast moustache—his friends call it a Los Angeles smog filter—shares with Art Katz a liking for books and good talk. But the similarity ends there. For unlike Art, Hal grew up loving his Orthodox Jewish faith. He loved the rabbis, the bar mitzvah, and even the tiny, awkward, skull caps.

Hal's life was guided by one supreme prayer —that his Jewishness might merit a keen revelation of God. Though a humble person by nature, Hal prided himself on his Jewishness. He sought a close walk with the God of Abraham. When he did not find that closeness in the synagogues of Los Angeles, he refused to foster personal resentment against the synagogue members. He merely concluded that the emptiness in his soul was the result of his own failings. But still he longed—and still he remained faithful. His Jewishness was precious to him. If there *were* more to add to it, then Hal was confident he would someday find it.

At the same time, there were other things to think about. Hal was pursuing a career in the television arts. While working his way through college, he found himself laboring beside another Jew. This man was quietly but clearly a vibrant, happy Jew. They became close friends. For weeks, Hal watched every move his new companion made. At all times, in every situation, whether pleasant or not, his friend radiated a calm peace and a powerful joy.

"I was dumbfounded," Hal confessed. "What did this man have? What did he know that I didn't?"

When Hal finally got around to asking him, his friend fondly replied, "It's not *what* I know, Hal, but *Who*. I know God."

Hal was stunned. He knew God, too. Wasn't he a Jew? He had been painstaking in his devotion toward God. Yet what he saw in his friend, he knew he lacked. He saw a love and a peace that was incomprehensible.

It was at this juncture that the two men were hired as assistants in the television production, *Jesus Christ Solid Rock*. In the company of producer Cal Habern and Pat Boone—as well as the cast of "Jesus freaks"—Hal again was moved by the love that surrounded him. And he was relieved that no one had tried to convert him.

Later, Hal's friend invited him to a dinner lecture. Having nothing better to do, Hal agreed to go. The dinner was at a downtown Los Angeles hotel and seemed innocently Jewish. But much to Hal's contempt, he discovered that the main speaker was a Jewish believer in Jesus. When the man began to speak, Hal turned red with anger.

"He's a turncoat, a traitor to his Jewishness," he thought. "Give me half a chance to speak to him, and I'll sure straighten *him* out! He might as well be Hitler! That *goy!*" °

Hal did get a chance to talk to the man. But the Spirit of God had already taken hold of Hal. When he met the speaker, he found him-

---

° *Goy* is a Yiddish term which means both heathen and Gentile.

self speechless. The speaker counseled him with a loving revelation of scriptural truths. Hal wanted to deny it all, but somehow he couldn't. Several Jewish believers present at the gathering were able to convince him that it was not necessary to stop being a Jew in order to follow Jesus. Hal's anger subsided, and his spirit broke under the tremendous weight of God's glory. That night Hal added a new dimension to his Judaism. Jesus became his Lord and Messiah.

He later wrote the lead article in *Yeshua ha' Mashiach*, a Messianic magazine. The full text of that article, reprinted here, will help to explain Hal's strong compulsion to communicate God's good news.

"It is our divine Commission . . . to bless the world with a consciousness of God."

If there is anything that all mankind might agree upon, it is that the world is in short supply of compassion. Science has broken through the barriers of outer space but can do little for inner space—the human mind. If a man has no will to care, technology can do little for him.

What has caused this vacuum among mankind? I believe it is because God's chosen mouthpiece, the Jew, has been all too silent. It is our divine commission, so much more than any other evangelizing or proselytizing movement, to bless the earth with a consciousness of God. We are God's communicators.

It was for this purpose that God called out Abraham our father:

> "Now the Lord had said unto Abram, Get thee out of thy country, and from thy kindred, and from thy father's house, unto a land that I will shew thee: And I will make of thee a great nation, and I will bless thee, and make thy name great; and thou shalt be a blessing: . . . and in thee shall all families of the earth be blessed." (Genesis 12.1,2 [sic])

Again and again Genesis repeats this commission: Isaac hears it at Gerar, Jacob hears it at Bethel. In Deuteronomy the Jew is challenged to be the spiritual light of the world:

> "The Lord thy God will set thee on high above all nations of the earth . . .
> And all the people of the earth shall see that thou art called by the Name of the Lord . . ."
>
> Deuteronomy 28.1,10

The commission later becomes the message of the prophets:

> *"I will also give thee for a light to the nations, that my salvation may be unto the end of the earth."*
>
> Isaiah 49.6

The implications of our divine call are so many that we cannot afford to overlook them. One would think that the reason our world is reeling in darkness is obvious: The Jewish star burns all too dimly. Are God's people, the Jews, interceding, witnessing, and praying for the soul of the world? If we do not communicate God to humanity, then we can only expect gross darkness. *"If they speak not according to this word,"* wept Isaiah, *"it is because there is no light in them."* (Isaiah 8.20)

We are in the age of advanced communications. High speed full color presses, television, radio, recordings, and telephone all send their messages out to the world's multitudes. We now have the technical know-how to beam out God's compassionate Word to every corner of the globe. But do we have the desire to do so?

We Jews cannot escape our responsibility. Jesus said to us two thousand years ago, *"Ye are the light of the world."* Our God is patient. But if all his witnesses remain silent, he will have to raise up others who are more willing. The Psalmist David proclaimed, *"The Lord is my light."* (Psalm 27.1) Where is our light today?

JESUS MADE ME JEWISH

Mike Evans

WHEN YOU have a Jewish mother and a Gentile father, it's like having matzo balls and pork chops on the same lunch plate. Especially when your mother is as Jewish as Golda Meir! I grew up in a kosher Gentile home, loved but confused.

People used to tell me to go to church, so I did twice a week. The Catholic church had bingo on Friday nights and the Protestants had dances on Saturday nights. I liked bingo and dancing. In my eyes I was as churchie as any Gentile. Besides, what more was there to Christianity than going to church? I had no comprehension of the *Ruach ha'Kodesh* (Holy Spirit) at all. As a matter of fact, one time my dad and I went to a Pentecostal church where they were praying in a strange language. Dad said that was of the devil and he prayed that the fella would choke.

I had no knowledge that for thousands of years Jewish people were clothed in the supernatural. Miracles were a way of life and the radiance of God's *shekinah* (glory) was ever in their midst. I never knew that the power of God was the heartbeat of Israel.

Everything was going my way. At nineteen I had a black belt in Karate, a new car, and a pocket full of money. Little did I know that I was about to come face to face with the *Ruach ha'Kodesh* of God and get shaken right out of my tree. I had just left Korea after spending fourteen months there with the U.S. Army. I returned to the States and was stationed in Philadelphia as a medical assistant at the Broad Street recruiting station.

One night, however, I became bored with it all. I drove aimlessly about the city by myself. Suddenly the idea hit me to drop in at some church and get acquainted with the girls there. Seeing a lighted church building, I pulled the car to the curb, got out and walked the darkened sidewalk back to the church.

Inside the building, everything seemed light and warm. There was something inviting, something divine about the whole situation. Up front, a big man of Russian descent was talking. He was a jeweler who obviously thought he knew God personally. He spoke very convincingly about God and man. I supposed that the Jesus he talked about was a business partner of his.

Suddenly God's *Ruach ha'Kodesh* came upon me. I felt like garbage, rotten! And I was aware of my sins as never before. I felt like an ax was cutting away at the core of my being. My whole life was before me and I began to shake uncontrollably.

After the concluding prayer, the speaker came to offer me encouragement. Aware of my uniform, he put his arm around me and said, "It must be hard being a Christian in the Army." "I really wouldn't know," I replied, "I'm not a Christian."

At that point, the man shared with me some words Jesus had spoken:

> Behold, I stand at the door and knock: if any man hear my voice, and open the door, I will come in to him, and will sup with him, and he with me. (Rev. 3:20)

This was my moment! I wanted to know God in a real way. I prayed and asked Jesus to be my Messiah. Suddenly He was very real. I broke and wept quietly, then bubbled over with joy.

I actually felt the presence of God all over me and for the first time in my life I was glad I was Jewish. I wanted to pray for Israel and for all my Jewish people. I could truly identify with Isaiah's cry, "The Spirit of the Lord is upon me."

Almost instinctively I began to pray to God as my heavenly Father and His presence came upon me like a mighty wind. Miracles began happening, first with a dear friend who had multiple sclerosis, then with a man that was crippled with arthritis. They were both healed of their infirmities.

Wow! I realized that I was in communication with the God of the now, the God of miracles. Some time later while driving home from Arkansas, I asked God to have a woman, who was over fifty miles away, pray for me for I was sick. Within five minutes I was completely healed and several days later when going through the town where this sister lived, she came up to me and asked me where I was at a special time and day. I told her and it was the exact time I had asked God for her prayers. On another occasion, we felt impressed to ask for a van in Little Rock, Arkansas, to claim it for the work of the Lord (the owner was not home at the time). Five weeks later when we were going through Little

Jesus Made Me Jewish

Rock again, the owner said that God told him to give us the van. Another time as several young Jewish believers were preparing to leave for New York to share the Messiah, we got on our knees praying that God would meet their expenses. We thanked God for hearing our prayers and a half hour later I went to the Post Office and in our mail there was a check for fifteen-hundred dollars! It was from a lady who lived over 1500 miles away, somewhere we had never been. The letter said, "this is for the New York ministry, God told me to send it."

Recently a man who had a cancer on his face asked me to pray for him. "Dear God," I asked, "in the Name of Yeshua ha'Mashiach, heal this man." Three days later the cancer fell off. A woman who was deaf in one ear was instantly healed through prayer in the Name of the Messiah.

Recently while on our trip to Israel, near the Sea of Galilee, I talked with an Arab businessman for over two hours. He expressed his bitterness against the Jewish people; his folks had lost their properties in Jerusalem in 1967 when Israel took the Old City. Suddenly I felt a great love for this man. Then I found myself inviting him to a prayer meeting. I didn't know of any prayer meeting, but the Lord directed us to my room to pray. He and I prayed, first for him, as he accepted the Messiah, then for all the Jewish and Arab people in the world that they might have peace! That "meeting" lasted four hours!

On another occasion I picked up two Israeli paratroopers who were hitchhiking to Jericho where they were stationed. As I asked them if they believed in God, they angrily responded that God died with the six million in Germany. I had no idea what to say, but before we reached Jericho their faith was restored in God through their new found Messiah, Yeshua.

The Messiah has given me the burden to pray for Israel and all my beloved Jewish people. Recently I asked a noted Orthodox rabbi about the *Ruach ha'Kodesh* of God. He admitted that it was real in the Old Testament, that miracles and mighty wonders happened. He said that he really didn't understand why it was different since the times of Malachi. But I can truthfully say that it is not different for me. The same living God that blessed the prophets of old is blessing me in the same way. His Son Jesus has brought this once lonely Jew so close to Him that I can now proclaim that the God of Abraham, Isaac, and Jacob is the God of Mike Evans as well!

THE GOD WHO LED ABRAHAM

Sarah Schneider [pseudonym]

I WAS brought up in an Orthodox Jewish home. My parents were both in concentration camps during World War II, and they learned what it was to suffer as a Jew. Out of a family of 150 closely related, only five survived under Hitler.

My father came from a Chasidic background. His father had a long beard and was very strict with his children. My mother came from a wealthy home where she was an only child. Her family, unlike my father's, was not Orthodox. I remember hearing her say countless times, "Many people lost their faith in God during World War II, but that is where I found mine." From that point on, she was a religious Jew.

I was raised in New York in a predominantly Jewish neighborhood. My parents were immigrants from Switzerland, and I was born a month after they landed. As a child, I went to Hebrew parochial school (yeshiva), where I learned the fundamental teachings of Judaism. The indoctrination was thorough, and I never thought there could be any other possible way of life. I was happy, secure, and I was taught to have faith in God and to look for the coming of the Messiah. Frequently I asked how we would know when He was coming and what heaven would be like, but I never got any answers.

At the age of twelve, I began to rebel. Because I was an Orthodox Jew, I couldn't associate with the boys and girls who hung around on the street corners at night, or be friendly with Gentile people in my neighborhood. This confused me; I did not understand why.

I became very rebellious in school, and the teachers didn't know what to do with me. Although the rebellion was very evident, the reason for it remained hidden. Looking back now, I can see that it was frustration, resulting from wanting to trust in a God that I had been taught about since I was a small child, yet not being able to know Him. As I sat in Torah class, I would listen very attentively, because I wanted to know this God who led Abraham, who gave Sarah a child when she was ninety years old, who made the Red Sea split in half for the children of Israel. Who was this God? What did He have to do with me? Why was I so frustrated and alone?

Whenever I asked questions in class, I was looked at strangely, or was told not to question, just to believe. I honestly wanted to, and I tried, but it was impossible. In my rebellion, I began smoking cigarettes and was such a terrible influence on my classmates that one day I was expelled from school.

I was petrified. What would I tell my mother? I finally told her the truth. Naturally, she was upset.

Next I began attending public school and found it a relief to act just like all the other kids in the neighborhood. I didn't have to put up a front about being religious; I could do just as I pleased. I pleased to turn as far away from Judaism as I could go.

By the time I was fourteen years old, I was my own boss, coming and going as I pleased.

Nobody had any control over me. I let my parents know I didn't want their way of life. I would find my own way.

When I was sixteen years old, I became involved in the drug world. I ran away from home, free at last—or so I thought. In order to get money for enough drugs for myself, I began dealing in them. I was always just one step ahead of the cops, but I thought I had found my answer in drugs.

Still there was something that kept me reaching out for something mystical and eternal. I didn't understand the battle going on inside me, but I remember the feelings I had at that time.

You see, what a person learns as a child always remains with him, no matter how far he strays. The feeling I had about God had never left me. Although I didn't believe, yet there remained a subconscious desire to really *know* Him. Not even the drugs could let me escape from that.

After a few years of drug pushing, I settled in a hippie commune in the desert of California. I was really just biding time—I didn't know what to do next.

One day a girl came out to the desert and

The God Who Led Abraham 47

began to tell me about Jesus Christ. I thought she was crazy. "Look, girl," I said, "I don't want to hear about no Jesus." I added that I wanted to know the truth about life. She told me how He *was* the Truth, and I scoffed some more. Finally, she left.

At that time, my boyfriend became quite interested in this Jesus, and he told me that he was going to go to the girl's house to ask her some questions about Him. I thought he was crazy, too, but when he asked me to go with him, I went.

I was dirty, barefooted, my hair was straggly, my clothes filthy. It was easy to see that I had been hitchhiking on the road for days. But the first thing I sensed when we got to the girl's house was not condemnation, but love!

I had never known love, real love. I had always wanted it, but I had never felt it as I felt it at the girl's house. I was not going to let it go.

We spent the night, and the next day the girl took us to church with her. I had never been to a church before, and it was a strange experience, so different from the synagogue.

Some of the workers in the church tried to talk with me about Jesus, but the more they talked, the more I clung to my philosophies. When we went back to the house, part of me wanted to leave, but I couldn't let go of that love.

Barbara, who owned the house where we were staying, gave me some tapes to listen to. She made me realize that there was a spiritual warfare going on inside me and that I needed to know Jesus in order to really know God. I began to think, "Well, either Jesus Christ is real, or He isn't. It's got to be one way or the other. There are no two ways about it." If my search was intelligent and sincere, I would have to look into this. A person truly searching cannot live with a doubt; he will have to investigate every solution he encounters.

"I'm going to find out if Jesus is real," I said. "If He's real, I've got to do something about it. If He's not real, I want to get Him out of my mind and never have to think about Him again. But I've got to find out, one way or the other."

When I went back to the church that night, something kept tugging at my heart. I couldn't go in the building. I wanted to, but I couldn't. I finally walked into the parking lot and began to cry. I cried out all the tears of loneliness, all the tears of misery I had bottled up inside since I left home. I was so miserable. Where could I turn?

I finally raised my hands up toward the sky and cried, "God, the Father of Abraham, Isaac, and Jacob, I know about You. I studied about You in school, and I know You are real, but what about this guy Jesus? Is He really Your Son? Is He really real? God, if Jesus is Your Son, You can tell me about Him. God, if You tell me about Jesus, I will follow Him. I want to do what is right, but I don't know." I continued to cry out, "God, I'm a Jew, and I need a sign tonight. I can't wait any longer. I can't keep on living with a doubt in my heart. Please, please show me."

When I walked into the church, I didn't hear one word of the sermon. I didn't understand what was going on. It was a big church, and at the end of the service when the pastor invited people to come forward to receive Jesus, something in my heart kept saying, "Go up front. Go up to the front of the church."

I argued with the something inside me. "That's silly. I can't get up out of my seat. People will look at me. I'm dirty and ragged. People will laugh at me."

But the something inside kept insisting,

"What do you care what people say? You've gone through too much to care about that. You've come too far to have to worry about them."

Suddenly I couldn't hold back any longer. I literally ran down the aisle. The pastor lifted his head as if God had spoken to him, and he said, "She just came home." Then he looked at me and started to cry.

"Praise the Lord," he said.

"Praise the Lord," was the first thing that came out of my mouth.

And then I heard God speaking to my heart. "Jesus *is* real," He said. "He *is* My Son. Follow Him from this day on, and He'll never lead you wrong. There are a lot of things you won't understand at first, but trust in Him. Hold on to Him. Believe in His name, and He'll see you through. He'll explain these things to you slowly."

I knew I had come home. Great peace, great joy, such as I had never known before, flooded my soul. At that moment, I understood that it was God's love that had captured my heart in Barbara's home.

I gave my life to Jesus, and I told Him, "Lord Jesus, I am a nobody. I'm nothing, and

I've been so miserable. Please help me. Change my life."

I know my life was transformed that very moment. I was saved from myself. I had met God at His fullest—through His Son Jesus Christ. The Scripture, "I am the way, the truth, and the life: no man cometh unto the Father, but by me," became so real to me because I had spent so much of my life searching for God.

Afterward, some Christians took me into a room and prayed that God would fill me with His own Holy Spirit. I told God that if it was needful, I wanted to have it. When I closed my eyes and began to pray, I felt the filling, and I began to praise God in a language I knew nothing about. I left that church the happiest person in the whole world.

THERE WAS THIS GIRL

Jeffrey H. Allen

TOWARD the middle of September, 1968, I was traveling back home from a brief vacation in the Catskills. Suddenly, without any warning, in that bumper-to-bumper traffic, at least five hours from my home in Rhode Island, I became absolutely deaf. It was the most horrifying experience of my life.

I turned the radio on full blast—and heard nothing. I was petrified. Grimly driving ahead, because there seemed nothing else I could do, I finally reached home. I got out of the car screaming at the top of my lungs, "I'm deaf! I'm deaf!"

Soon I was stretched out on a table in a doctor's office. He inserted a device in my nostrils, and kept pumping away at a big rubber ball attached to the end of it, trying to draw the congestion out of my head. As a result, I found myself on the operating table on Rosh Hashanah, the Jewish New Year.

After the operation, I was thrilled to be awakened by the sound of a telephone ringing, but my emotions plunged as I felt the sharp pains caused by the tiny plastic drainage tubes inserted behind my eardrums. Every time I swallowed, drank, coughed, sneezed, or did anything else, the tubes would shift position in my head, causing my ears to ache unbearably.

I was also given a very powerful decongestant with instructions not to drink when I was taking it, not to drive or do anything else requiring an alert mind.

In April of that same year, I attended a fraternity party and caught a glimpse of a girl far too pretty to be with the brother who was her escort. By the end of the evening, I had Cindy's name, her telephone number, and my own motives—which were far from pure.

Before many weeks had passed, I had fallen deeply in love. And then I received a letter out of the clear blue:

"Jeff, I never want to see or hear from you

again. Please, don't call or try to see me. It will only upset things. I don't feel that I could ever live up to your expectations—"

I had considered myself a cold, dispassionate being, but upon reading those words, I threw myself on the bed and wept until my pillow was drenched with tears.

Drained and weak, as if a knife had ripped open a wound and I was hoping death was not far, I read on, nauseated at the next words that came off the page:

"Jeff, I believe we were brought together for you to come to know Jesus Christ as your Lord and Savior."

I could not believe what I was reading! For a minute, I tried to pretend the words were not there. What could this Jesus Christ have to do with the girl I loved? It was bad enough that all through school, I had been the object of every low and jealous scheme of those goys. All this had added to the inherent hostility that Jews have toward the one in whose name we have suffered beyond description for two thousand years.

What could this sweet girl possibly have to do with such things? This question haunted me for the next two years.

During those two years, my life took a decided turn for the worse. I was not satisfied with my position in life, deeply resenting the affluence of my family because of my utter dependence on them. In my rebellion, I began to go to places where one would never expect to find a well brought up Jewish boy. I became all too familiar with the streets of New York, Boston, Newark, etc. Females were playthings with no feelings. Life was a miasma of filth and wretchedness, filled with sleeplessness, anxiety, animosity, the unending pain from the tubes in my ears and an ulcerated stomach.

On my birthdays, during that period of time, when my parents would ask what I desired or where I wanted to go, I invariably replied, "I would like to go to sleep tonight and never wake up again."

"Jeff, why do you say these things to us? It's like twisting a knife in my belly," dad cried.

"I say it because it's true, and I'll never find peace any other way," I answered him.

In the meantime, I continued to live life at two hundred miles per hour, finding no satisfaction nor any one thing that could get my attention long enough to slow me down. I became more and more convinced that in death was the only peace. And surely the peace of death was preferable to the torment of life.

The last day of January, 1971, I picked up the prescription in Providence. I remember the druggist eyeing me suspiciously, asking if I wanted the whole quantity, seeing how strong and expensive the dosage was. Riding back to Narragansett, where I was enrolled in school, I was mustering the courage to take not just one of those capsules, but all of them. Tonight, I said to myself, the abstract thought of death is going to become a physical reality.

Forty miles away, someone was listening to a different voice. Cindy, who was in hairdressing school at that time, sat studying when suddenly a vision of my face appeared before her with the voice of the Lord, saying, "Cindy, if you don't call Jeff Allen tonight, you will never see him again *alive*." Trembling, she picked up the receiver to call my Jewish home, knowing that in the past my parents had not approved of her. The first time the phone rang, my mother answered and did not respond to her questions. Cindy called again, with even greater urgency, and received much the same lack of response from my father. Thank God, my sister answered the third call and told Cindy where I was.

I was pulling myself away from the dinner table when the phone rang. My roommate, Jeff Klienman, answered. I'll never forget the words I heard when he handed the phone to me:

"When you hear who this is, promise you won't hang up?"

I promised, asking, "All right, who is it?"

"It's Cindy."

"Cindy!" All thoughts of suicide vanished from my mind in that moment. It would be two weeks before I could see Cindy, because her schedule was so crowded, but I could wait. During that interval, the Lord was preparing me. I felt hope surging, and the filthy sediment of my thoughts and actions settling somehow. I became like a little child, not quite believing that something so wonderful could actually happen to me.

That Friday night finally arrived. I had spent days in preparation, even to the point of cutting my hair just like it had been two years before. I didn't want Cindy to know what I had become.

There were no words to express my joy at seeing her again. Later I learned that God had filled her with His Holy Spirit since we had last seen each other, and now she had the boldness to say what she could not say before. All day she had been praying, "Lord, make an opening."

Suddenly, in the midst of our talking, Cindy began to weep, relating to me a painful relationship that had just ended for her because a boy set in his playboy philosophy could not reconcile himself to walk in the same light that she had found to be real. I felt sorry for her sorrow and wanted Cindy to be happy tonight, so I, for whom the tears were actually shed, began to comfort her. At the end of the evening, she invited me to attend a Full Gospel Business Men's banquet where a Jewish evangelist would be speaking.

"What's a Jewish evangelist?" I asked her.

"Oh, that's a Jew who has accepted Jesus Christ as his Lord and Savior," she said.

Once again I felt the nausea begin to roll in my stomach. I had heard stories of forced conversions, and remembered how weak I had thought those Jews were to accept an alien God rather than lay down their lives for the God of our fathers. But since Cindy was asking, I agreed to go.

As I left my room the night of the meeting, my roommate said, "Don't get yourself involved in anything you'll be sorry for."

I assured him there was no danger of that, because I had to get in early to write a major paper due on the teacher's desk by nine the next morning. It would take me all night to complete it.

As I listened to the speaker, Art Katz, giving what he called his "testimony," all the filthy thoughts, all the vile actions of my life prior to the last few weeks came to the surface. I almost choked on them, I was so uncomfortable. I couldn't understand this sudden anxiety. Why should I be upset? I was with the girl I loved—

That Jew—if ever I had seen or heard one before, Katz was one—was relating his encounter with this Jesus Christ about whom I was hearing so much lately. I heard him give an "altar call," and people streamed up for prayer. When they came back to their seats, I had to admit they seemed somehow illuminated.

But the inner voice to which I was accustomed to listening said, "You don't need this. You're strong, intelligent, rich—"

For an hour, I was bound to that chair, unable to move, arguing with myself, and then, finally, another voice broke through, saying, "There will never be a moment like this moment again."

Knowing the voice spoke truly, and that I could leave all the filth and grime of my life behind me in the chair, I charged forward. In my usual egotistic style, I heard myself say to the speaker, "Say, you think *you've* got a story—why don't you listen to mine?"

In moments I heard myself confessing things in my life that I had refused to admit to myself, and then, in the midst of it all, this same Jesus became so real to me, with His arms out, waiting so patiently for me, that I received Him that very moment.

Art said, "Jeff, you're going to sleep like you've never slept before."

But Satan was not about to let go so easily. After we had returned to Cindy's home and shared my joy with her parents, my head began to fill with congestion, just as it had on that long road two years earlier. Cindy's voice grew ever so dim, and I could feel the pain scrawling itself over my face. Could my joy be finished so quickly?

"What's wrong?" Cindy's parents asked.

When I told them about the pain and the

deafness, they approached me and laid hands on my head, saying, "In the name of Jesus, clear his head."

POP! My ears opened, the pain was gone, and I could hear perfectly. Two weeks later, I realized I had no need for pills to keep my ears open. The pain from the ulcer was all gone, too.

Then I remembered the paper I was supposed to write, and I knew I had neither the time nor the energy to complete it. Again a prayer was offered for me:

"Lord, You know his need. Please take care of it for him. In Jesus' name."

I have no recollection of the forty-mile trip back to school at 1:15 A.M. nor of sitting down to write that paper. All that I do know is that I was in bed sleeping by 4:15 A.M., and the next morning I handed the professor a paper entitled "Logic and the Scientific Method."

Two weeks later, the professor handed papers back to everyone in the class except me. When I approached him about it, he asked, "Is your name Jeff Allen?" I nodded. "You had better come to my office to see me as soon as possible!"

Wondering apprehensively what it was all

about, I skipped my next class and went to his office immediately. By the time he arrived, I was stuck to the chair with perspiration.

"Mr. Allen," he began, "I have never before received a paper of such magnitude or caliber on this topic. I'm sorry, but you could not possibly have been responsible for writing it. Now, tell me—who wrote it for you? Or from what source did you copy it?"

My mind was a blank, and for a moment I was speechless. Then I ventured to defend myself:

"But Sir, I did write that paper. I can show you my original notes, and—" I was blank again.

"All right, let me quiz you on it. The author of your main text, what was his name?"

"I can't remember. Let me think—" The silence was deafening.

"Well, Mr. Allen, you know this means an F in the course and possibly grounds for dismissal. We just can't stand for plagiarism in this school!"

I could not believe the nightmare of what was happening. Then I thought back to that night and remembered that simple prayer, "Lord, You know his need." I prayed it again,

"Lord, You know my need," and my memory was immediately restored, so that I could quote freely from the paper.

The professor's jaw dropped, and he apologized for his accusations. Then I looked him square in the eye and said, "Sir, you were right the first time." There was no backing away now. I had to go through with it. "Sir, Jesus wrote that paper for me."

The professor became the first with whom I shared my testimony.

One day after receiving Jesus, I was sitting at a table with Cindy and her mom listening to them tell me that God was going to use me in a ministry to my people. Then they said that just as Jesus told His followers to wait until they received power from above, I would need this power also, to be a witness to the Jewish Messiah. They did not tell me all that was involved, so I put up no intellectual barriers. We simply held hands in prayer, and suddenly the Baptism in the Holy Spirit was mine—and I was speaking in tongues.

Now I had the power—and the evidence of it—I needed to face the next task, speaking to my parents about Him.

Whenever in the past I had returned home from school, the tension could literally be cut with a knife. This time, I came in with the new love I had found.

For three weeks, it seemed as if I was getting nowhere with them. I was up against what I call "The Jewish Mother's Rap." My mother was confusing my going out with Cindy with converting to another religion. I tried to assure her this was not the case at all, but she couldn't understand.

One Saturday afternoon I was talking to mom about her own need to find peace for her life, and I could see she was embarrassed with this talk of a personal God. We concluded with a prayer for the return of my sister who had for six months been away from home, her whereabouts unknown. The very next morning, she was at our front door, asking to come in!

Later I felt the Lord's leading to write my parents a letter about all that had happened to me. I assured them of my love for them, and confessed my foolishness in mistrusting them when I could have gone to them for help. I told them that the physical miracles of healing they had seen in my body were nothing compared to the miracle of the truth God had revealed to me—that Jesus came into the world to give life and life more abundantly, and that except a man be born again, he cannot enter the Kingdom of God. I agreed that the Old Testament was the law, but that in Jesus we have fulfillment of the law.

Needless to say, I was apprehensive about mailing the letter, but as I told Cindy, my parents were open-minded, and if they could put up with such a one as I had been until now, one who more often than not brought humiliation to them, then they would surely see how wonderful what had happened to me really is.

But they did not see it at all.

When my parents received that letter, they took it to a psychiatrist who wept along with them. His analysis was that I was "tripping," and at the end of the trip, I would find severe disillusionment or worse. Although my parents had recognized a new stability in me, and had even remarked at my apparent overnight maturity, they agreed with the psychiatrist.

It was as if they could accept the clay that the Potter had prepared, but not the Potter Himself.

Their next step was to take the letter to a

lawyer, and I was legally disowned. Their son was dead.

When I returned home the next time, I was told what had happened. Their stand was firm. I was no longer their son. I was told never to come back, to return the keys to the house, and to give them back my new car.

My mother spoke her hatred for me, and that it would have been better for her to have heard from Vietnam that I was never coming home.

My father pointed his finger at me and uttered words by which I choose to live: "Go sleep with your Jesus, and see what He does for you!"

Art Katz's words echoed in my memory: "Jeff, you're going to sleep like you've never slept before."

I left humbly that day, thanking my parents for all they had done for me. Closing the front door behind me, I threw my hands up toward heaven and said, "Daddy, I'm all Yours."

When I picked up my Bible, I read Psalm 27:10: "When my father and my mother forsake me, then the Lord will take me up."

Then I read Jesus' words in Luke 18:29-30: "Verily I say unto you, There is no man that hath left house, or parents, or brethren, or wife, or children, for the kingdom of God's sake, Who shall not receive manifold more in this present time, and in the world to come life everlasting."

The day Cindy and I met at the altar, I looked up at a beautiful mural of the empty cross with just the crown of thorns left, and I imagined the One whose visage was marred more than any man and what He had done for me. Together, Cindy and I said, "Lord, whatever You require, we shall do."

MY KINSMAN ACCORDING TO THE FLESH

Menaham Ben-Hayim

MY PARENTS, Hyman and Rebecca, were a young immigrant couple when they moved to the United States from a small town in Eastern Europe in the first decade of this century. Reared in the strict Orthodox Jewish tradition that has changed little during centuries of restricted life in Eastern Europe, they had to make tremendous adjustments, not only to a new country, but also to a new age. It was natural that they tried to preserve as much as they could of the old tradition.

Amid the crowded tenements of New York City's Lower East Side, my parents reared seven children, of whom I was the youngest. By the time I was ready for school, the family had advanced enough economically to leave the narrow streets, the unheated tenements, and the shared privies of the ghetto. We could afford a flat in the ampler areas of Brooklyn, and eventually central heating and a gas range, a private toilet and bath.

I grew up during the depression years prior to the outbreak of World War II. My companions were mostly children of Jewish and Italian immigrants of working-class background.

I used to think that mankind was divided into two races—the Italians and the Jews. Walking home one afternoon with a six-year-old Italian school chum, I somehow entered into a religious dialogue with him.

"Did you know, Pasquale, that our God made the world?" I proudly informed him. I had started studying the Hebrew Scriptures at an early age, so for me, Genesis was an elementary fact. My young Roman Catholic companion thought about that very earnestly for a moment, and then solemnly countered, "But our God made the streets!" That was a profound theological challenge to a city child. For the moment, I could only remain silent, and walk along trying to grasp the significance of it.

I was educated in the public schools of New York City, graduating from high school in June, 1941. After the United States' entry into World War II, I joined two other brothers in the Service. Assigned to the Medics, I served for three years, in the United States and in England.

Like most children of Orthodox Jewish immigrants, I had by this time abandoned most of the old traditions and regulations which we identified with an outmoded ghetto way of life. "This is the twentieth century," we were all saying, overlooking the fact that it was a century still numbered from the birth of Christ.

It was during this period that the novel *The Nazarene*, by the Yiddish writer, Sholem Asch, appeared. It created a sensation, and great controversy. Many Jews bitterly attacked Asch for his sympathetic portrayal of "Rabbi Yeshua," while others defended his attempt to re-Judaize Jesus for both Jews and Gentiles. In a Brooklyn synagogue I sometimes visited, a prominent rabbi devoted two weekly lectures to the novel—before large audiences.

It was not too long afterward, while I was serving in England, that the novel came to my mind again. I thought that a man like Sholem Asch, reared in traditional Judaism, emancipated, a Socialist, identified with his people, yet a man of the world, could help me to understand this strange Jew of Nazareth who loomed so large in the history of mankind. So it was that in 1944 I went rather furtively into a small town near my army base to buy my first complete Bible. I had decided that I would first have to study the source of the *The Nazarene* before I could evaluate the novel based on it.

I still remember the joy I felt at reading the Sermon on the Mount and the parables of Jesus. How thrilled I was at the teachings of the great Rabbi of Galilee, my "kinsman according to the flesh." I committed large passages of the New Testament to memory. I was really moved by the humility of Jesus' life and teachings, and how He admonished the disciples against the desire for status and show of authority.

> Ye know that the princes of the Gentiles exercise dominion over them, and they that are great exercise authority upon them. But it shall not be so among you; but whosoever will be great

among you, let him be your minister; And whosoever will be chief among you, let him be your servant. Even as the Son of Man came not to be ministered unto, but to minister, and to give his life a ransom for many. (Matt. 20:25-28)

Truly, I thought to myself, this was the ultimate in Jewish teaching. What objection could any right-thinking Jew have to it, whatever he might think of the churches in Christendom?

I became convinced that *if* there was any basis for a Jewish Messianic hope, it could only have been fulfilled in Jesus, our own Rabbi Yeshua, from whom "we hid, as it were, our faces . . . and we esteemed him not" (Isa. 53:3).

For a long time, I hid my face from Him, too. But eventually I realized that I could not indefinitely escape the necessity for a full and open commitment to Jesus Christ.

I knew that accepting Him and acknowledging Him openly would not make me any less a Jew inwardly. It would rather be a completing of my Judaism, "a circumcision not made with hands," and my fulfillment as a member of the people God had chosen for His special purposes. Yet it was extremely difficult for me, deeply rooted in Jewish life and culture, to take such a drastic step. In the eyes of most Jews, such a commitment represents a severance from the life of Judaism.

For a number of years, I visited from time to time various assemblies in the fragmented Christendom of our time. I was naturally drawn to the more liberal groups which seemed to be in the least collision with my situation as a rather liberal unaffiliated Jew. I also became involved in many good works, from such conservative ones as the American Red Cross to such unusual ones as the "Catholic Worker." The latter was a radical Catholic group with a pacifist social-action philosophy and program. I was especially drawn to their ministry toward the poor and outcast.

Aflame with activity and interests, reading much, writing (I edited a small inter-racial bulletin in New York City for part of a year), I was in contact with many people in the hectic life of the city.

In private conversations, I had become willing to express my belief in God and in Jesus as Messiah and Savior. But I always took care not to seem "too religious" or "fanatical."

Suddenly, in the midst of this whirl, I felt a clear call in my mind and heart to proclaim

My Kinsman According to the Flesh 75

such faith as I had openly and unreservedly. I hoped the call would go away, but instead, it became even more intense. I began to shun most of my old sophisticated friends, as I could not communicate with them. Finally, I had to undergo a complete reorganization of my life. Out of the severest crisis of my existence emerged a clear and open confession of faith in Jesus as the Christ, and a willingness to identify with those who shared this faith, whether Jews or Gentiles.

During this period of crisis, I met R.F., a Hebrew-Christian who was director of a Jewish mission on the Lower East Side. He had come out of a strict Orthodox Jewish background in prewar Poland. In Warsaw, he had been led to a saving faith in Christ just a short time before the outbreak of World War II. His entire family had perished in that holocaust. It was through R.F. that I met other Hebrew-Christians in the area.

After a year of fellowship with them, I was baptized in the Atlantic Ocean as a simple act of identification with the death and resurrection of our Jewish Messiah.

Later that year, on the eve of the New Year, 1961, I met Haya, who lived in a small town in southern Connecticut. Three years from the time that I had made a full and open confession of faith in Christ, Haya and I were married in the home of Jewish believers in Connecticut.

My wife and I were both active in testifying to our faith among our Jewish people and among Gentiles. After a year in Connecticut, we moved to Miami Beach, Florida. In this area, sometimes called "Little Israel," there were several Hebrew-Christian groups in the midst of a heavy concentration of Jewish population. I found employment as a surgical orderly at the County Hospital, and we were both very happy, enjoying great liberty of speech and activity.

Both my wife and I had always had a deep love for Israel. As a youth, I had been active in several phases of the Zionist movement in America, which was then working toward the establishment of a Jewish state in Palestine. As believers, however, I felt my wife and I were neither young enough nor strong enough to undertake the challenge to settle in Israel. Many of our people were convinced that their greatest enemies were Christians. To their way of thinking, the Nazis were Christians, as was anyone who was not a Jew or a Moslem. In their eyes we would seem like traitors who had joined the camp of a vicious enemy.

But the same God who visited our fathers in their weakness and afflictions lives today. After definite assurances of His continuing providence, we made arrangements for sailing to Israel on an Israeli freighter, leaving from Miami harbor. On March 17, 1963, we reached Haifa.

There we stayed briefly with R.F., who had come to Israel as Israeli Secretary of the International Hebrew Christian Alliance. In the spring, we moved into a kibbutz, a collective settlement, in Lower Galilee. Our faith and testimony were made known to those around us, and we were surprised at how little hostility was directed against us. We cannot say there was any great enthusiasm, but there was a considerable amount of interest and attempts to comprehend such unusual species of Jews as we appeared to them to be.

In the autumn of that same year, we settled in Eilat, a small, newly developed town sandwiched in on the edge of the great Negev Desert to the north and the Sinai Peninsula to the south. To the east lies the beautiful Red Sea shore, and on the far side of that shore the Arab port of Aqaba, connected with the exploits of the famed Lawrence of Arabia. Here we have lived and labored for over seven years.

Basically, the non-believing population is tolerant of us. We are welcome in many homes, and can often bear witness to our Lord and Redeemer among the ingathering exiles of Israel who have come from the far corners of the earth—Jews from Yemen, India, and Shanghai, to the east; Jews from the Americas and Europe, to the west; Jews from South Africa and Ethiopia; from North Africa, from the British Isles, and North Europe. Truly, we are participating in the great historical miracle long ago foretold in the Scriptures:

> For I will take you from among the heathen [Gentiles], and gather you out of all countries, and I will bring you into your own land. . . . And ye shall dwell in the land that I gave to your fathers; and ye shall be my people, and I will be your God. (Ezek. 36:24,28)

In our small way, we bear a living witness to the fact that "God has not rejected his people [Israel] . . . for the gifts of God are irrevocable" (Rom. 11:2,29). We are standing on the same ground as the Jewish followers of the Lord Jesus in the days of the New Testament.

We believe that the God of our fathers who was manifest so perfectly in Yeshua, our Jewish Messiah, will yet be recognized fully by His own people. Hallelujah!

I WAS "GAY," BUT NOW I'M HAPPY

Alan Greenberg

HOMOSEXUALITY, despite the great increase of public attention it has attracted in recent years, remains a dark mystery to most people and a nearly unmentionable sin among Christians. The Bible records Jesus' forgiving the adulteress, the thief, and even the very soldiers who were nailing His sinless body to the cross. But nowhere do we read that a homosexual sought or was granted His pardon. Does this mean that this sin is so unspeakable and so filthy that even the blood of the Lamb cannot suffice to wash away its shame? God forbid! I know that Jesus loves the homosexual, because He sought me when I was trapped in the "gay" life and made a new creature of me. Praise His name!

I was brought up in a Jewish middle-class home where God's name was heard more often in an oath than in a benediction. My sister and I were taken as children to the local synagogue but that came to a stop before I reached the age of bar mitzvah. Ours was a home rich in material blessings, but very deficient in family love, and altogether ignorant of the surpassing love of God.

The signs of emotional disturbance showed up earlier in my sister than in myself. Before she was sixteen, she had run away several times and was continually in trouble with the school and civil authorities. In my own efforts to submerge my feelings of loneliness and anxiety, I became an impassioned student and won several scholarships which enabled me to attend a fine university.

I "came out" as a homosexual at the age of twenty-one. I had just broken an engagement with a childhood sweetheart, and my sister came to live with me in my apartment in New York. She had already entered the "gay life" as a teenager, and now she introduced me to her friends.

In a short time, I was caught up in the illusory glamour and excitement of the homosexual half-world. I went to the private clubs and "cruised" all night in the streets or in the bars. Drinking was part of the atmosphere, and I wanted all the pleasure I could get. From the beginning, I had wanted a stable relationship with another man, but I soon found that homosexuals are not able to love, but only pretend to love. I began to pretend, too, and in order to bring myself to indulge in so much promiscuity and pretense, I drank more and more.

The hunger in my heart for real love was never satisfied, even though I did have some affairs that lasted several months each. Meanwhile, I had finished college and two years of graduate school, and had taken an excellent position as a librarian in the City College of New York. I had lost so much of my self-respect that I concealed my homosexuality only from my professional colleagues. More and more I was despairing of ever finding love in my life, and often I had to struggle against a powerful suicidal urge.

In July 1970, I went on a vacation to Europe, intent upon having as much pleasure in one month as I could. I spent my days in museums and libraries and my evenings in bars and bathhouses. On August 2, the last day but one of my vacation, I met K., in Copenhagen. As I had done so many times before, I went home with a man and spent the night with him. Two desperate souls had found one another, and instantly "love" sprang up between us. I promised to write, and a passionate correspondence ensued. Driven almost mad by my new devotion to K., I suddenly gave up my position at the library, sold all my furnishings, and flew to Copenhagen on September 14, 1970.

Our romance lasted scarcely a week before we discovered that neither of us was capable of loving at all. All we could do was to demand love from each other, loudly and selfishly. While K. was at work, I wandered the streets of Copenhagen, crushed, disappointed, bewildered. I had gambled everything and lost. I was in a hell of remorse and hatred.

All my efforts to find work in Denmark were unsuccessful, and K.'s demands for money did not end with my arrival in the country. As a last measure before admitting failure to my friends and to myself by returning to New York, I decided to try to find work in Great Britain. I wrote to a great number of firms, and succeeded in making a few appointments for interviews. But then my spirits were so low. I didn't really care about a job very much, and spent most of my time in London in the Humanities Reading Room of the University of London Library. There I enjoyed the collection of fine literature by authors of every nationality, and for hours I lost myself in the world of the imagination.

One day my eye was caught by a volume called *What I Believe* in the collected works of Leo Tolstoi. Knowing Tolstoi only as a master novelist, I was curious enough to open the volume. There I read words that burned in my heart, and I found answers to questions that I had never dared frame in my mind: What is the purpose of man's life on earth? What is the meaning of death? What does Jesus Christ have to say to a frightened man in an industrial society of the twentieth century? Suddenly He said to me, "Come to me ye who labor and are heavy laden and I will give you rest," and my dilemma didn't matter to me anymore. I knew nothing about this Christ, and yet in my heart of hearts I knew that He spoke the truth. With that tiny scrap of truth, I fed my starving soul, and leaped with joy as one risen from the dead!

I soon returned to New York, not defeated and ashamed, but filled with hope. The Lord led me to a mission to the Jews on 72nd Street in a building I had passed on my way to group therapy sessions for two years and had never even seen! There I heard the whole glorious Gospel and gave my life to the Savior who had revealed the glory of God to me in my darkest moment.

The Lord has led me through many trials and many triumphs since that day in December 1970, including the unspeakable joy of the Baptism in the Holy Spirit in August 1971. I felt as if I would be swept into eternity by the overwhelming power of God's love, but instead I was borne up into a higher and purer walk with God. Where once was the bitterness and grief of sin, there is now a contentment in my soul and the sweet fellowship of the saints. There have been temptations in the last two years, but through Christ my homosexual lusts have been thoroughly defeated.

In February 1972, I met a wonderful girl, a sister in the Lord, whom I married in June. God has blessed our union in the most wonderful way, and we look forward to a life together in the service of the Messiah.

THE LOST SHEEP OF THE HOUSE OF ISRAEL

Abraham Eilezer

I WANT to tell you how I found Jesus in my heart and life, and what He did for me.

I was born into a family of Orthodox Jews in Azerbaijan which is between Turkey and Russia. Both my father and my mother are Cohens—Cohen is a Hebrew word for "priest" —and my ancestry reaches back to Aaron the High Priest. We were exclusively Jewish in all religious matters, and during my childhood and adolescence I had no contact with anyone who believed that Jesus was the Messiah.

When my parents began to see Jewish people returning to Israel, they were very happy.

Moving to Israel had long been their dream, too. They knew from the Bible that God had promised this land to the Jewish people. And in 1951, when I was two years old, they moved to Israel to claim their share of it.

Years later, a neighbor friend of my parents invited me to go with him to a Bible study. "I'm sure you will like it," he said. I agreed to go with him and really did enjoy it very much. But after a few more meetings, I began to realize this was not the Jewish Bible as I knew it, but a new Bible of some kind. They were teaching from the New Testament, which we Jews considered the Gentile Bible. I decided they were trying to trick me into false teaching, and so I did not attend the Bible study again.

When my friend questioned me about my absence, I told him I did not want to study any new Bible, only the Jewish Bible, the Old Testament. I told him further that if my parents found out I was going to the Gentiles to study the new Bible, they would kill me. My friend was very understanding, and for a long time, he did not bother me.

After two years, he came to me again and said, "Do you know that Jesus, the Jewish Messiah, loves you very much and wants you to accept Him into your heart? Please come to the meeting again. You can find Him there."

I didn't realize it at the time, but of course this was the hand of God. He would not give up on me, but wanted to give me another opportunity to find Him as my personal Savior and Messiah.

I said to my friend, "Why did your Jesus send you again to me?"

He said, "My Messiah and your Messiah are the same, and He sent me to tell you we are going to study the guitar today."

I said to myself, "I will learn to play the guitar and then leave them."

After a few weeks, the guitar teacher said to me, "I want to give you a little gift. I am sure you will find something important in it for you."

I went outside and opened the package. I felt sick when I saw what was inside. It was the New Testament. Afraid that my parents and my friends would see it, I cut the book in pieces and threw it on the road.

Later, the teacher asked me how I had liked the book. I lied, and told him I didn't know where I had left it. When he replaced it with another copy, I asked myself what would happen if I opened the book and tried to read it. One day, I did just that.

The New Testament contained many wonderful things that I had never heard before. In the reading, my eyes were opened, and I found Jesus, my Messiah! Oh, how happy I was! I believed He would come again some day, and I was so glad I had found Him and He had found me.

About this time, I began to have a bad relationship with my family and friends. One by one, they all shunned me, until I had no one but Jesus. He was everything to me, and was with me every moment during this trial of my faith.

One day my parents said to me, "You are a grown man, now. You are old enough to know what you are doing. Do what you want to do. And God be with you."

Two weeks later, the Six Day War broke out. I had been out of the army for two weeks, but I went back in to drive a tank. It was very dangerous duty, but I was not afraid, because I had Jesus my Messiah watching over me. I knew that all His promises are Yea and Amen to us that believe in Him, and that He had promised to be with us even unto the end of the world. I had read in the Word of God that though a thousand should fall at my right hand, and many on my left, God would protect me just as He protected King David of old. I was praying to Him all the time, and He brought me out of the danger without a scratch.

And, just as God watched over me, He also protected this whole nation. Before the Six Day War an old man went through the streets of Jerusalem prophesying exactly what would happen and on what day the conflict would begin. He said the God of Israel lives today and promised that He would be with Israel and His Jewish people through it all. The events that old man prophesied came to pass. God fought for Israel during the Six Day War; otherwise, with so many soldiers against us, we would never have won.

After the war, some of my comrades told me that in one area of combat, our forces had advanced so rapidly that they overran an Egyptian airfield in the Sinai peninsula and were in full possession before the Arab allies could be notified. So, when the unsuspecting Arabs phoned the field, offering to send in Algerian fighter planes, our man simply pretended to be an Egyptian officer and authorized the planes to land. Every one of those planes was captured without the firing of a shot.

But the most interesting story came from soldiers we captured during the Sinai campaign. We asked one, a veteran of the war between Egypt and Yemen, why he had given up the fight so quickly. He reported that he and his comrades had seen angels coming at them from the Israeli lines and had fled in terror back toward Egypt. Truly God intervened on behalf of our tiny Jewish nation.

After the war, I began praying that God would send me a good and faithful wife who would believe in Jesus as her Messiah so that together we could work for His glory in the land of Israel. Hannah is God's answer to that prayer. When I first spoke to her about Jesus, it was very hard for me. With the Lord's help, I said, "I want you also to ask Jesus to come into your heart." She did it gladly. Today she is ready for the time when God makes a way for us to go into full-time service for Him here among the lost sheep of the house of Israel.

AND GOD SAW THAT IT WAS GOOD

Anne Goldman [pseudonym]

ANNE GOLDMAN is the kind of pleasant Jewish girl who brings to mind the biblical Esther. She is quiet, unassuming, and at nineteen, the epitome of tranquillity.

Anne grew up in Chicago in a Reform Jewish family. She attended Sunday School at Temple for ten years and went to services occasionally on Friday nights. During her junior year of high school, she worked as a volunteer children's counselor at the neighborhood YMCA.

This volunteer role at the YMCA was to have a great effect on her life. It was while she was working there that she met Mike Evans, who introduced her to Messianic Judaism. Anne thought it was absurd for a Jew to believe in Jesus—she did not even believe such a man had ever existed.

On vacation in Hawaii, Anne heard again about Jesus from another young Jesus person. Her first thought was, "Oh, no! Not here in Hawaii, too! I can't get away from it!" But she listened to him, and he gave her a Bible which she took back to her hotel to read.

All during her travels throughout the Islands, Anne kept thinking about Jesus. For the first time, she wanted to know more.

As soon as she returned to Chicago, Anne telephoned Mike Evans. He invited her to a gathering of Jesus People. All through the meeting, Anne prayed silently, "God, if Jesus really is Messiah, please reveal Him to me." At the conclusion, everyone, including Anne, knelt for prayer. In simple words, she accepted Jesus as her Messiah, and at that instant, a warm, glowing peace filled her life. She started praising God and thanking Him for revealing Jesus to her. Before she knew what was happening, she heard herself speaking in a language she did not understand. She only knew it was a language of praise to God.

After her powerful encounter with the Holy Spirit, Anne went out determined to tell the world about Jesus. Her parents, needless to say, were quite upset and concerned about her. They decided to send her to a psychologist, and, in time, the tension in her home forced Anne to decide to move out. But to Anne Goldman, Jesus is worth it all.

THE MOVEMENT SPREADS

MESSIANIC JUDAISM is gaining momentum everywhere. It is even possible to find a few longtime rabbis who are now ardent spokesmen for the movement.

Michael Esses is one such man. The author of *Michael, Michael, Why Do You Hate Me?* Esses is one of the most popular lecturers at the Melodyland Christian Center in Anaheim, California. This man is impeccably Jewish. He was raised in an Orthodox Sephardic background, the son of a rabbi who headed the largest congregation of Judean Jews in New York City. Esses was educated in a New York Yeshiva, and was eventually ordained to the rabbinate. Today he commands large audiences wherever he speaks. Invariably, Jesus is his topic.

On the East Coast, another rabbi, a young Air Force chaplain, testified on the campus of the University of Maryland that he is now a "completed Jew," a follower of Messiah Jesus.

Other Jewish evangelists and leaders of Messianic cell groups have had to fill the role of rabbi whenever one was not available. Manny Brotman, a young leader of the Beth Shalom congregation in Miami, conducts an orderly Hebrew service. One man who dropped in on the worship services came away saying, "You would think they are still Jews. But then again, I guess that's what they are supposed to be."

That is Brotman's whole point. "When a Jew comes to trust in Messiah Jesus," Brotman explains, "he doesn't want to cease being a Jew and start being a Gentile. He has no desire to turn his back on his invaluable heritage. He is a Jew forever."

In order to evangelize strictly on Jewish terms, Manny Brotman has founded the Messianic Judaism Movement International. Almost every Jesus Jew in the country agrees with Brotman on one point: to reach the Jew, you evangelize, not proselytize. While the proselytizer seeks to convert people from one group to another, the evangelist stirs up passions for truths that are already imbedded within a group, but lying dormant.

Almost nothing is said about *converts* among

these Jews. This was the fatal mistake of Protestant denominational missions programs in their efforts to "reach the Jews." Workers in such programs could not conceive of an individual who could accept Jesus as his Messiah and still remain a Jew; Christians were Gentiles and Jews were Jews, and between the two groups there was a great gulf fixed. Consequently, they labored hard to get converts, but all of their best programs met with only scant success. It has been only recently that people have realized that Jews could love and follow Jesus and still remain Jews.

Martin "Moishe" Rosen of the American Board of Missions to the Jews was one of the first to take this point of view. In fact, his San Francisco group has been using the slogan "Jews for Jesus" for quite some time. Recently the group plastered the campus of the San Francisco State University with red stickers bearing this slogan.

Some of the most eye-appealing tracts for programs in Jewish evangelism come from this group. Steffi Geiser, a twenty-one-year-old Jewess, turns out most of their poignant but simply illustrated tracts. Many other "Jews for Jesus" groups include someone whose full-time work it is to produce such material. Many groups send out newspapers bearing such Jewish names as *Manna, The Shofar, Shalom,* and *Messiah.*

So far, no one has felt the need to unite the various worldwide groups into a single organization. But there is no lack of unity among them. "The thing that unites us is our Jewishness and our love for Jesus," says one University of Colorado Jewess. The Young Hebrew Christian Alliance (YHCA) is one of the better known of recently formed Jews for Jesus organizations. The YHCA sponsors campus gatherings, especially on Hanukkah and other Jewish holidays. These gatherings provide an opportunity for non-Christian Jews to hear about Jesus. In Philadelphia, a young bearded chemist, Joe Finklestein, is YHCA chairman. The group he heads meets regularly at The Hidden Matzoh, a large house-turned-meeting-hall.

But for all this, the price that some Jewish young people pay for accepting Jesus is staggering. Many are thrown out of their homes by their families, and completely abandoned by their friends. Some of them have had to face the ironic fact that while they were rebellious drug addicts, they were at least tolerated. But when they found deliverance in Jesus, they were scorned and shunned.

Yet all of this has not slowed the enthusiastic movement in the slightest. Rabbi Michael Esses recently encouraged a group by long-distance telephone. "Don't let it worry you," he spoke reassuringly, "for Jesus said in Matthew 24 that we would encounter great opposition for His sake. It's all a part of the plan—a part of prophecy. But we are in to win. Our brothers and sisters are at stake."

Someone on the other end replied, "Praise Jesus!" and the conversation turned from concern to jubilation.

There is no turning back for these Jews who have declared for Jesus. They are like their father Abraham who, in answer to God's call, ventured into the unknown. The price they have to pay is precious and lonesome. They, too, must leave their father's house and go to an unfamiliar land.

Some Jewish parents still write off their "Jesus children" as dead. However, this practice is not as widespread as in times past, because many of the parents themselves are non-religious. Still, parents who are devout Jews react strongly. Many a young Jew for

Jesus has found himself disowned by his family.

And yet, happiness is the byword of this movement. Almost all testimonies of the Young Lions speak of overflowing joy. The same thing was true of the very first Jesus movement two thousand years ago. Those early believers were some of the most persecuted Jews ever. Yet Simon Peter described their experience as "joy unspeakable and full of glory" (I Pet. 1:8). This same Peter referred to these believers as "strangers and pilgrims" (I Pet. 2:11).

Indeed the Messianic Jews *are* strangers and pilgrims. Their Jewish friends no longer consider them Jews: but neither are they Gentiles. It will be interesting to see what will become of this people who now stand in the middle. They have heard the call and forsaken everything to follow Jesus. The words of Peter might well be their own rallying cry: "Nevertheless we, according to his promise, look for new heavens and a new earth, wherein dwelleth righteousness" (II Pet. 3:13). In this hope, they are truly sons of Abraham, standing in faith and calling others to citizenship in the Kingdom of God.

The Jewish move toward Jesus is vastly important in the fulfillment of last-day prophecy.

The Movement Spreads

According to God's promise in Isaiah 49:6, the Jew is His timepiece and light for the world. They are His chosen people, and the continuing means by which He reveals His will to the world.

Joel prophesied that with the rebuilding of Israel, a great spiritual renewal would occur among the Jews:

> And it shall come to pass afterward, that I will pour out my spirit upon all flesh; and your sons and your daughters shall prophesy, your old men shall dream dreams, your young men shall see visions. (Joel 2:28)

The very last spiritual awakening—before the end of time—foreseen by John the Revelator was among the Jews. He was told that 144,000 Jewish believers in Jesus were to be presented before the throne of God. These "Jews for Jesus" will be gathered from all twelve tribes of Israel. We know that this ingathering signals the very end, for it is followed by Antichrist's massive invasion which plunges the world into World War III.

Even during the period of Antichrist's occupation of Jerusalem, two Jewish witnesses will openly defy him. They will proclaim the Gospel and work great miracles in the streets of that city (Rev. 11:3). Many prophets speak of this period as a time of pleading the rest of Israel into the new covenant which Jesus offered. Ezekiel, for example, follows his prophecy of a rebuilt Israel with a sudden turn of events:

> And I will bring you into the wilderness of the people, and there will I plead with you face to face. . . . And I will cause you to pass under the rod, and I will bring you into the bond of the covenant. (Ezek. 20:35,37)

Israel will learn that she can no longer trust merely in her political leaders. Ezekiel warns, "There is a conspiracy of her prophets" (22:25). "They shall call on my name," Zechariah hears the Lord proclaim, "and I will hear them" (13:9).

Israel was rebuilt not to be merely the homeland of the Jews, but to become a lighthouse for the world. "And nations shall come to your light," Isaiah predicted, "and kings to the brightness of your rising" (60:3 RSV).

Only then will the covenant which God made with Abraham, father of Israel, be fulfilled: "Thy seed [shall be] as the stars" (Gen. 22:17).

AN AFTERWORD: JEWISH CULTURE AND IDENTITY

Joseph Finkelstein

ONE of the great enigmas facing Christians today is the Messianic Jew, the Jew who, while he has fully accepted Jesus as his Messiah, nonetheless wishes to retain his Jewish cultural identity. In times past, Messianic Jews have been discouraged from maintaining their Jewishness because Gentile Christians felt that the Jewish believer might "slip back into his Judaism" and abandon Christ. Others have maintained that since all Christians are now "one in Christ" there is no need for the Jew to be much concerned about his culture or heritage.

An examination of Old and New Testament

Scripture, however, suggests that this cultural separation is warranted but should produce unnecessary separation in sympathies and outlook between believing Jews and Gentiles. Indeed, Scripture would suggest that respect for the Law and the Prophets is basic to the Christian life.

The New Testament repeatedly demonstrates its dependence upon the writings of Moses and the prophets. In John 1:45, for example, Philip declares to Nathanael "We have found him [the Messiah], of whom Moses in the law, and the prophets did write, Jesus [Yeshua] of Nazareth." In the parable of Dives and Lazarus, the rich man pleads with Abraham that he might send Lazarus to warn his five brothers to mend their ways. But Abraham replies, "They have Moses and the prophets; let them hear them" (Luke 16:29). Yeshua challenged his kinsmen to "search the Scriptures" (the Tenach, or Old Testament). He continued, "For had ye believed Moses, ye would have believed me; for he wrote of me. But if ye believe not his writings, how shall ye believe my words?" (John 5:46-47) He Himself declared that He had not come to destroy the law or the prophets; rather He had come to fulfill them (Matt. 5:17). Later, on the walk to Emmaus, the risen Yeshua "beginning at Moses and all the prophets . . . expounded unto them in all the scriptures the things concerning himself" (Luke 24:27). Philip began with the book of Isaiah when he witnessed to the Ethiopian eunuch (Acts 8:30-35) and Paul, as is recorded in Acts 17:2 and 28:23, taught from the Law and the Prophets both in the synagogue and in his own lodgings.

We can clearly see that the message of salvation for everyone, Jew and Gentile alike, is a Jewish one. The Jew comes first, and the Gentile comes second. This is why Paul compares the Jews to a natural olive tree, and the Gentiles to branches of a wild olive tree that have been grafted onto the natural tree (Rom. 11:13-24). Thus the question that is so often asked of us, "How can you be Jewish and believe in Jesus?" can only be answered, "Well, how can you be Jewish and not believe in Jesus?" The fact of the matter is, when one strips away the traditional hostility of Gentile Christianity toward Judaism, there remains a pure Jewish message for all who would call upon the God of Israel in spirit and in truth.

Since the Scriptures clearly demonstrate the

Jewishness of the Gospel, what is the relationship of the Messianic Jew to his specifically Jewish customs, traditions, and even the Law of Moses? Is he to discard them, as some might expect him to do? Is he to consider them irrelevant to his new experience? Or, on the contrary, may he hold on to them, and discover in them, because he is a Messianic Jew, a deeper meaning and significance? There was at least one Jew mentioned in the New Testament—among many others—who, while he was a follower of Jesus, nevertheless did not lose sight of his Jewish identity. His name was Paul.

Although Paul is best known as an apostle to the Gentiles, there are at least a dozen references in the Book of Acts alone that attest to the fact that he kept all the customs of the Jews. He *routinely* attended synagogues wherever he journeyed and, as we have already indicated, reasoned with his kinsmen from the Tenach. Acts 20:16 indicates that Paul still observed the Jewish feast of Pentecost and even arranged his missionary journeys to accommodate its celebration.

There were many Messianic Jews, Paul among them, who still observed the Law of Moses (cf. Acts 21:20, 24). On the surface, this would appear to be an exercise in futility, for if Paul preached anything at all, he surely emphasized the fact that works of the Law were of themselves powerless to insure salvation. Why bother with them, then? Let us examine this apparent contradiction.

If there was ever a man who knew that the works of the Law could never justify anyone, it was Paul. His letter to the believers in Galatia clearly demonstrates this fact. The Jerusalem Council, which included Paul, ruled that believing Gentiles should not be required to undergo circumcision, nor keep the law of Moses, but should only abstain from the pollutions of idols, fornication, the eating of any strangled animal, and the eating of blood.

These proscriptions served a dual purpose. Not only did they separate the Gentile Christians from the pagan practices that were going on around them, but they also indicated an expression of solidarity with Jewish Christians, since these four prohibitions were ones about which the Jews were particularly sensitive. Nonetheless, the Council did *not* tell the believing Jews who still kept the Law of Moses to cease from their practice. Nowhere in the New Testament is the Messianic Jew forbidden to observe Jewish customs or the Mosaic Law if he chooses to do so. There is only the warning (and it is a very sound one) that such a Jew should not expect his observance to place him in any better standing with God.

What is it, then, that influenced Paul and many other believing Jews to keep their ancient customs and the Law? They retained them because they passionately desired to see their Jewish kinsmen experience the abundant and fulfilling life that God wanted for His people. Seeking to speak to the brethren in such a way that they would clearly understand and identify with his message, Paul declared in I Cor. 9:20, "And unto the Jews I became as a Jew, that I might gain the Jews; to them that are under the law, as under the law, that I might gain them that are under the law."

This was not some sinister attempt to seduce our people into accepting Yeshua as their Messiah by "using" Jewish customs or the Mosaic Law. Paul wanted his brethren to see that it was Yeshua who completed these customs and the Law, and fulfilled the meaning of Jewish existence. He wanted, both by his words and actions, for his fellow Jews to see in him a "completed Jewishness," and he wanted them to desire this for themselves (Rom. 11:14).

A perfect scriptural example of how a Messianic Jew went to his people as a Jew is found in Acts 16:1-3 when Timothy accompanied Paul on his second missionary journey. Since Timothy's father was a Greek, he had never been circumcised, and the Jewish people of Iconium and Lystra whom Paul and Timothy sought to evangelize knew this. Timothy, of course, had all the freedom in Christ to remain uncircumcised, but so as not to offend the Jewish people and to keep lines of communication open, Timothy submitted himself to be circumcised.

We can learn much from his example. If Timothy was willing to endure physical pain so that he might more fruitfully share his Messiah with the Jewish brethren, Messianic Jews, indeed all believers, of today should similarly ask themselves what sacrifices could be made in order to more effectively communicate the message of salvation to friends and family.

Christian emblems, churchy catchphrases and exclamations, even ways of presenting the Gospel that offend or humiliate our parents and co-workers can be sacrificed so that unnecessary barriers between Jews and believers are not erected in the name of freely expressing new life in Christ. This can be a difficult task where church norms seem to demand "proof" of Christian loyalty, but in the end it will lead to a better understanding of what it really means to serve and worship God in spirit and in truth.

If we are honest with ourselves, we will agree that, from scriptural and practical considerations, Jewish cultural identity is still a significant factor in the life of the Messianic Jew. As a factor in our witnessing to other Jews who do not yet know Yeshua as their Messiah, it is indispensable. Until we give definite evidence of our Jewishness to our non-Messianic brethren, they will quite rightly believe that we have left our heritage behind and are now no more than *goyim*. But as they get to know us and are guests in our homes, as they see us quietly and reverently observing the same customs and holidays that they observe, then they will be ready to look into our lives to see the fullness and joy that Yeshua gives, and will be more open to receiving Him themselves.

Recently, my wife and I entertained our par-

An Afterword

ents for Shabbat dinner for the first time since we had received the Messiah. When Debbie and I first accepted the Lord, they were tremendously resentful and antagonistic, so we wanted this dinner to be one of reconciliation as well as testimony. Debbie and Rachel, my daughter, lit the candles. I said the Kiddush and Rachel did the blessing over the bread. She's five years old and knows the whole prayer in Hebrew by heart. Our parents were taken aback. They couldn't believe what they were seeing. Debbie and I could see God at work changing their hearts just by their reactions to that Shabbat visit.

It is no coincidence that Yeshua made some of His most profound statements on Jewish holidays. On the Feast of Succoth (Feast of Tabernacles), for instance, He made two statements which can be fully savored only in the light of Jewish customs.

On the last day, the great day of the feast, Yeshua stood and cried out, saying, "If any man thirst, let him come unto me and drink. He that believeth on me, as the scripture hath said, out of his belly shall flow rivers of living water" (John 7:37-38). During the celebration of this feast, one of the Jewish priests was sent to draw water from the Pool of Siloam. The High Priest then poured the water and a pitcher of wine into a basin at the foot of the altar. Yeshua's declaration referred to this solemn moment in the feast, and pointed his people to the fact that only He could truly satisfy their spiritual thirst.

Then Yeshua spoke again, saying, "I am the light of the world; he that followeth me shall not walk in darkness, but shall have the light of life" (John 8:12). This statement is much more meaningful when we realize that for the Succoth celebration, the Temple in Jerusalem was greatly illuminated both inside and out. Yeshua again sets his great promise for spiritual fulfillment in the context of a beautiful Jewish feast. He links his claim to be the light of life with the inspiring scene of the Temple, surrounded on Succoth with the glow of thousands of flickering lights.

Even at the Passover Seder, the intensely moving dinner of deliverance established by God thousands of years ago, Christian believers find themselves right at home. From the outset of the meal, participants will see three pieces of unleavened bread (matzoh) are placed on top of one another. These matzohs, according to Jewish tradition, represent, from top to bottom, God, the mediating high priest, and the people.

The head of the Seder must break the middle matzoh (which represents the mediating high priest) in half, wrap one half in a linen cloth and hide or bury it. During the meal, it will be stolen by one of the little children and redeemed for money by the head of the Seder. He then breaks the returned matzoh into as many pieces as there are people present at the meal, and everyone eats a piece. All that remains is an empty linen cloth. This section of the Seder is a dramatic symbolization of the death of the Messiah, and is an antecedent of the Christian Lord's Supper. It is performed yearly in almost every Jewish home, though without any explanation of its meaning.

Study of the scriptural pattern of witnessing to Jews and our own experiences have confirmed to us that as we respect and draw on our Jewish Law and culture rather than abandoning it as "unchristian," God is able to break down many barriers between believers and non-believers. As we demonstrate a genuine love for our Jewish brethren, they will begin to see that we Messianic Jews are still very much Jews—but Jews who have found the fullest sense of their Jewish identity in Israel's Yeshua ha'Mashiach.

Please address all letters and comments to:

MIKE EVANS
P.O. Box 14327
Fort Worth, TX 76117